Celtic Christmas
COLORING BOOK

CARI BUZIAK

DOVER PUBLICATIONS
GARDEN CITY, NEW YORK

Celebrate Christmas with 31 enchanting Celtic designs. Santa Claus, reindeer, wreaths, ornaments, Christmas trees, and other festive holiday symbols are beautifully accented with traditional Celtic flair, including knotwork, spirals, and other classic motifs. The images are printed on one side only, and the pages are perforated for easy removal and display of your finished artwork.

Bibliographical Note

Celtic Christmas Coloring Book is a new work, first published by Dover Publications in 2021.

International Standard Book Number
ISBN-13: 978-0-486-84697-2
ISBN-10: 0-486-84697-0

Manufactured in the United States of America
84697001
www.doverpublications.com

2 4 6 8 10 9 7 5 3 1
2021